Being Crazy

NEHEMY N. KIHARA

ISBN:1539146006
ISBN-13: 978-1539146001

DEDICATION

To my maternal Aunt Felicia Wacuka Gathogo Weru-Kago
And all like her; struggling and fighting gracefully
the problem of 'Losing Memory'
To all my cousins-Mwangi Weru; Kago'Reki' Weru;
Kabiru Weru; Macharia Weru, Githaiga Weru
and their families for taking care of Mama.
To all those that society has declared 'crazy' and
all that suffer from mental illness
To all persons ,families and professionals that
dedicate their efforts and at times unrecognized .service
to people considered to have gone or 'going or being crazy. .

CONTENTS

ACKNOWLEDGMENTS

My acknowledgements go to
the Kenyan Department of Health
and the Division of Mental Health..
The Health Education Network and all those working in Wards at
Nyanza/Kisumu General Hospital, Nyeri General Hospital and
Nanyuki Hospital
Least but not last all Mission /Church Hospitals and
Community Counsellors...

1 INTRODUCTION

Now, that Kenya is about to embark on the formulation of a comprehensive mental health care system. Insights from anthropology will definitely be found useful, not only in operational, preventions but also in promotions research and education.

"Kenya is a cosmopolitan country overtaken by many psychosocial vicissitudes such as;, disintegration of our traditional institutions, rural-urban migration, longer life expectancy, rapid population growth rate, unemployment, socio-economic problems, alcoholism, drug abuse, AIDS, and the list is endless ... Anecdotal notions suggest a rising psychiatric morbidity most of it preventable" (Re: Kenya Mental Health Program for the next 10 years and beyond p. 1).

The Kenya Vision 2030 envisages a globally competitive and prosperous Kenya. The health sub -pillar of the Social Pillar seeks to invest in the health of the people through the restructuring of the health delivery system and shifting the emphasis on the-:

- Promotion of primary health care and treatment of diseases at community level,-

- Encouraging Kenyans to change their lifestyles in ways that will improve the health status of individuals, families and communities and

-Establishment of community based health information systems.

This will make the nation prosperous , ease its disease burden and deal better with such neuropsychiatric disorders and mental disorders such as unipolar depression, bipolar disorder, schizophrenia, epilepsy, alcohol and drug use disorders, dementias, anxiety disorders and mental retardation

-Alzheimer & other dementias

-Drug dependence & problem use

Briefly stated a decentralized, comprehensive and integrated Kenyan Mental Health Care model and the "expected devolved model" which involves such things as liaison psychiatry is overdue.

According to the Mental Health Act, 1989 ... (p. 11-12)

"A person suffering from mental disorder, means a person who has been found to be suffering which includes a person diagnosed as a psychopathic person with mental illness and person suffering from mental illness and person suffering from mental impairment due to alcohol or substance abuse.

The World Health Organization (WHO;2001:3) defines health as "not merely the absence of disease or infirmity", but rather, "a state of complete physical, mental and social well-being"

Moreover,

Mental health is defined by WHO(2010pg116) as "the successful performance of mental function, resulting productive activities, fulfilling relationships with other people, and the ability to adapt to change and to cope with adversity; from early childhood until later life, mental health is the springboard of thinking and communication skills, learning, emotional growth, resilience and self-esteem

Positive mental health as defined by WHO (2009) includes emotion (affect/feeling), cognition (perception, thinking, reasoning), social functioning (relations with others and society) and coherence (sense of meaning and purpose in life.

WHO (2003p7) further define mental health as, a state of well-being whereby individuals recognize their abilities, are able to cope with the normal stresses of life, work productively and fruitfully, and make a contribution to their communities"
"Person suffering from mental disorder" means a person who has been found to be so suffering under this Act and includes a person diagnosed as a psychopathic person with mental illness and person suffering from mental impairment due to alcohol of substance abuse;

According to Kenya Mental Health CAP 248(2012:Issue 1.)"Substance abuse" means the maladaptive pattern of use as indicated by either recurrent or continued use of any psychoactive substances (such as alcohol, amphetamines cannabis sativa, cocaine, hallucinogens, inhalants, opioids sedatives, hypnotics, or anxiolytics) where such use causes or exacerbates persistent or recurrent social, occupational, psychological or physical problems.

"Treatment" includes medical treatment, nursing and care and training under medical supervision.

Basically a person with an acute mental disorder is incapable of managing self is considered dangerous to self and others, is likely to act in a manner offensive to public decency.

We need therefore, to examine the Kenyan Mental Health Care and some related anthropological themes in the light of the sort of issues that are raised by the Mental Health Act, 1989.

Some insights from psychological anthropology (personality and culture) seem to yield some significant issues such as psycho-social universals, adaptations, normality and abnormality one

2 PSYCHOLOGICAL UNIVERSALS

1. According to French physiologists Claude Bernard (1813-1878) animals exists in two environments:

    (i)   an <u>external</u> milieu in which organisms is actually situation and

    (ii)   an <u>internal</u> milieu in which the tissue elements are present ... it is concerned mainly with the physiological and biochemical aspects of the organism.

Bernard (1865) concluded that the primary condition for freedom and independence of existence was the constancy and stability of the internal milieu and the mechanisms that allowed this state to continue.

According to him the organism had to be "so perfect that it can continually compensate for and counter balance external variations". The equilibrium had to be constantly maintained and all the vital mechanisms had only one object: that or preserving constant the conditions of life in milieu "interior".

2 .In the psychological environment, there is also an external and internal milieu (Pollock; 1961). In both we find definitive regulatory devices designed to deal with various alterations that may occur. When the nervous system had difficulty in dealing with increases in excitation through associative thinking or motor discharge, Freud and Brever (1892:27-30) suggested that a "psychical trauma" occurred.

Freud (1911) formulated in the "Two Principles of Mental Functioning" two modes of constancy adaptations: -

(i)the immediate energetic discharge or avoidance of the pleasure - pain principle and

(ii)the capacity, oriented to external reality, for discharge delay of the reality principle.

This later type of adaptation used mechanisms involving consciousness, attention, notation and memory storage as well as decision-making with action to alter external reality and thought, as a means of coping with new and potentially disruptive situations.

Freud's "psychological consistency" model parallel Bernard's Physio-biochemical stability model. In both the internal milieu was optionally maintained within a certain range.
Less variation could occur here in contrast to external milieu, and various defense mechanisms were necessary to maintain this consistency of the inside.

Cannon (1939) elaborated the concept of stability further by his principle of homeostasis which emphasized biological processes tending to re-establish steady states of equilibrium and constancy when disturbing elements upset the state of the balance.

Furthermore, various optimal ranges for particular processes have been discovered by biologists in the continual investigations. With disease interferences these ranges vary in accordance with the degree of impairment imposed upon the organism, as well as with the restitutive capacity operative within the organism.

Cannon (1939) envisioned the extension of his homeostasis idea to include "some general principles for the establishment, regulation and control of steady states" which could be applicable to social and industrial organization.

3 CAPACITY FOR ADOPTIVE RESPONSE

A fundamental property of every living organism, at every stage of its existence, is the capacity for adoptive response to its external environment which allows for a state of balance in internal milieu.

Cannon (1939) noted that the perfection of the process of holding a stable state in spite of extensive shifts of outer circumstances is not a special gift bestowed upon the highest organization but is consequence of a gradual evolution.

According to Darwin (1890) natural selections seems to have favored those individuals and species that possess the greatest power of responsive plasticity of the individual within optimal range of adaption.

Both of the theory of evolution and that of dynamic steady state or homeostatic adaptation are necessary to the understanding of human responses to psychological and physiological stress (both external and internal)

. We must have adaptation to the environment now and the capacity for it in future, if smooth functioning is to be secured.

Adaptation involves a series of processes that are goal-oriented and designed to facilitate establishment of a static equilibrium between the organism and its environment.

In some other situation the optimal level of equilibrium is fixed and various mechanisms attempt to adjust to this consistency. In other situations, devises are utilized to allow for a state as close to the optimal as possible.

In any event the adaptation process is a dynamic one, having its roots in the biological structure and constantly attempting to balance intersystem tension by way of the ego (Hartmann, 1939).

Freud (1936) said that human beings utilize defensive maneuvers in psychological adaptations and located this within the structural organization of mental apparatus in the "Ego" and the "Id."

Freud explained the ego's integrative role and elaborated its relationship to the external milieu (reality) as well as to the (psychic) internal milieu. Freud (1936) developed further protective and sustaining aspects of the ego's function.

The ego's ability to perceive the reality of loss, to appreciate the temporal and spatial performance of this loss, to acknowledge the significance of the loss; to be able to deal with the acute sudden disruption following the loss.

To be able to deal with the fear of weakness, helplessness frustration, rage, pain, and anger; to be able effectively to reinvest new objects or ideals with energy, and to re-establish different but satisfactory relationships which are the key factors in the process of ill health.

The process has certain phenomena, utilizes certain mechanisms, and has definite end point. Pathological interferences with it results in maladaptation with resultant psychopathology.

The common mental disorders in Kenya and the World are ;

-Depressive disorders,

-Substance use disorders,

-Schizophrenia,

-Epilepsy,

-Alzheimer's disease,

-Mental Retardation and

-Disorders of Children and Adolescence.

Symptoms of these disorders are abnormal thoughts, emotions, behavior and relationship with others (WHO: 2003).

The International statistical Classification of Diseases and related health problems (ICD-10) defines the mental illness and disorders.in the following Broad Categories of Mental and Behavioral Disorders Covered in ICD-10

1. Organic, including Symptomatic, mental disorders – e.g. dementia in Alzheimer's disease, delirium.

2. Mental and Behavioral disorders due to Psychoactive Substance use- e.g. harmful use of alcohol, opioid dependence syndrome.

3. Schizophrenia, schizotypal and delusional disorders – e.g. paranoid schizophrenia, delusional disorders, acute and transient psychotic disorders.

4. Mood (affective) disorders- e.g. bipolar disorder, depressive episode.

5. Neurotic, stress-related and somatoform disorders- e.g. generalized anxiety disorders, obsessive-compulsive disorders.

6. Behavioral syndromes associated with physiological disturbances and physical factors - e.g. eating disorders, non-organic sleep disorders.

7. Disorders of adult personality and behavior – e.g. paranoid personality disorder, transsexualism.

8. Mental retardation – e.g. mild mental retardation.

9. Disorders of psychological development- e.g. specific reading disorders, childhood autism

10. Behavioral and emotional disorders with onset usually occurring in childhood and adolescence- e.g. hyperkinetic disorder, conduct disorders, tic disorders. (Adopted from WHO World Health Report 200

4 CULTURAL RELATIVISM: NORMALITY AND ABNORMALITY

Western ethnographic reports contain numerous examples of various kinds of behavior which is treated in their culture as symptoms of mental illness - which are regarded in other cultures (like ours - African-Kenyan) as unexceptional, normal or even desirable.

Therefore, as such mental illness seems a relative concept, dependent on culturally defined behavioral norms. What precisely this suggests is that `people said to be mentally ill in one culture would be found normal in another, and vice versa.

Furthermore, concepts of mental health thus understood, include subjective well-being, perceived self-efficacy, autonomy, competence, intergenerational dependence and recognition of the ability to realize one's intellectual and emotional potential.

A western diagnosis of abnormality, seem to regard inability to functions socially as a good indicator of mental ailments but regards this as a function of culture.

Some other communities see mental illness **as** any condition that seriously impairs, either temporarily or permanently, the mental functioning of a person and is characterized by the presence in the person of any one or more of the following symptoms:

- Delusions,

- Hallucinations,

-Serious disorder of thought form,

-A severe disturbance of mood,

-Sustained or repeated Irrational

-Behavior indicating the presence of any one or more of the above mentioned symptoms.

On the other hand, normality within a very wide range is culturally defined. It is primarily a term for the socially elaborated segment of human behavior in any culture; and abnormality, a term for the segment that their particular civilization does not use.

The concept of normality is created by human beings and is our own seeking and therefore, culturally defined. Every culture defines its normality and in dealing with abnormalities with universal sanities. The concept of normal is properly a variant of the concept of good.

Society approves a normal action in terms of its own limits of expected behavioral patterns which are considered to a great extent the culturally institutionalized type of behavior.

Kenya Mental Health Act (CAP248 M1511 Issue 1)   Defines the Society's power to take person suffering from mental disorder into custody

Any police officer of or above the rank of inspector, officer in charge of a police station, administrative officer, chief or assistant chief may take or cause to be taken into his custody—

(a) any person whom he believes to be suffering from mental disorder and who is found within the limits of his jurisdiction; and

(b) any person within the limits of his jurisdiction whom he believes is dangerous to himself or to others, or who, because of the mental disorder acts or is likely to act in a manner offensive to public decency; and

(c) any person whom he believes to be suffering from mental disorder and is not under proper care and control, or is being cruelly treated or neglected by any relative or other person having charge of him.

According to Benedict (1934) individuals have sets towards certain types of behavior and these sets run sometimes counter to the types of behavior which are institutionalized in the culture to which they belong.

In a society that institutionalizes or value `disrespect of the elderly' individuals will be disrespectful to the elderly. In a society that sets the gathering of possessions as the chief human objective, they will amass property.

The deviants, whatever the type of behavior the culture has institutionalized, remain few in number.

One universal fact remain, that the majority of humanity quite readily take any shape that is presented to them which means in turn that most individuals are plastic to the molding force of the society in which they are born.

5 PERSONALITY AND CULTURE

Some preliminary anthropological issues deemed necessary to the Kenyan mental health Care were raised in terms of the relationship between personality and culture.

Kenyan "society" and "culture" are a circular continuum. It is the individuals who make the "society" and, its "culture" exists on a psychosocial-behavioral level.

The Mental Health Act of 1989 become familiar to this author ,when he was invited by the Ministry of Health to 'Workshop' that dealt with issue pertaining to the provision of Mental Healthcare in the Kenya.

As an Consultant Anthropology and Social Scientist from Kenyatta University we represented the Academia, with ,another Sociologist from the University of Nairobi.

In this Act, much of what was discussed was issues pertaining primarily to the care treatment and rehabilitation and little mention of preventive and after care services such as counselling psychotherapy and vocational care.

 Mostly, more time was spent in discussions on

 -- Depression and Anxiety ,were seen as common mental disorders; better dealt with by local Communities ,both traditional and religious healers. While some have intensive experience and training, others seem to have very little of both.

-Alcohol and other Chemical Substance Disorders ,-treated at the District Hospitals and Provincial Hospitals ,when more severe.

-Epilepsy as well as dementia ,were the main Neurological Disorders mentioned ,as the ones treated at Provincial and National Hospitals .

-Psychosis, Schizophrenia and Bi-polar Disorders ,which were more severe, were often mentioned in discussions of the only public National Psychiatric Hospital, namely Mathare ,in the capital city of Nairobi.

There was more emphasis on treatment in hospitals of those with severe mental diseases, and little mention of the human rights of persons with mental illness; prevention or early intervention, or community involvement.

Most of other participants were the mental health care providers, who were serving as psychiatrists from provincial institution which were duly licensed and accredited under the written law of the Nyayo KANU Regime, for the time being in force to provide health care service.

The Kenya Mental Health Bill of 2014,was introduced in Parliament to repeal this 1989 Act .In the Bill,2014,25-27,mental health is defined as ' a state of well-being in which the individual realizes his or her own abilities, can cope with the normal stresses of life, can work productively and fruitfully and is able to make a contribution to .his or her community;'

Mental illness is defined as any illness or disorder of the mind; thus a person with mental illness is seen as a person diagnosed as suffering from a mental illness;

The relationship between the individuals their societies and cultures are reciprocal. Society is the organization of groups of individuals while culture is the organized group of ideas, habits and conditioned responses shared by members of society.

Without culture a group of people are not a society, but just a mere aggregate.

On one hand, stabilizing culture tend to reinforce the already established personality patterns than towards the evolving new patterns.

While on the other hand, a changing culture influences and differentiates between the personality and shapes the influences being experienced; which to the individual could be a disorganizing factor.

6 DIAGNOSIS

It is necessary, in Kenyan Mental Health to consider the psychosocial significance of the events that the individuals (persons) experience such as familiar organization, psycho-cultural internalization and structuralization.

Kenyan culture according to its major preoccupations will increase and intensify hysterical, epileptic and paranoid symptoms at the same time relying socially in a greater and greater degree upon these very individuals.

Variability of the "normal" in our culture and its consequences need to be realized, so as to rationally deal with inevitable change and the variability in time of the "abnormal".

The phenomena of living beings - especially humanity must be considered as a harmonious whole. – This holistic organism has a dynamic capacity for adaptive response to its external environment.

In turn this allows for a state of balance in its internal milieu (which have phylogenetic significance as well as ontogenetic importance);

Whereas, adaptation achievements may turn into adaption disturbances; the adaptive process should be understood to involve in part an undoing of the previous adaptational equilibrium and re-establishing of new relations with the reality present.

We have to realize that "the abnormal" is an individual upon whom a culture has put more than usual strain. His/her ability to adapt him/herself to society is a reflection of the fact that adaptation involves conflicts in him/her, which it does not in the so-called "normal".

7 PROGNOSIS

Benedict (1934): suggested that-

1. Therapeutically, relativity of normality suggests that the inculcation of tolerance and appreciation in society.

2. The complement of this tolerance on the patient's side is an education in self-reliance and honesty with him/herself.

3. Realize that

  (i) Despair at ones lack of social backing results into misery and mental illness.

  (ii) Achievement of independence and less tortured, oppressed or alienated attitude lays the foundations for an adequately functioning mode of existence.

May I close by stating that "individuals tend to give to culture in society what it has given them; while culture in society produces what the individuals have created

8 MENTAL HEALTH ACTS AND POLICY

The Mental Health Act of 1989 become familiar to this author ,when he was invited by the Ministry of Health to 'Workshop' that dealt with issue pertaining to the provision of Mental Healthcare in the Kenya.

The political context of the workshop was in accordance with the dictates of the period, any criticism of the Government including its Ministries were not to be entertained or tolerated.

However the shortcomings of the Ministry of Health and the National and Provincial Hospitals were obvious. From the local Health Clinics, Dispensaries and Health Centers, there were shortages of the basic provisions of hygiene such as plastic gloves, clean syringes and medicines.

In District now County level hospitals, all kinds of unhealth situations, existed in wards such as ones with patients suffering from severe TB,HIV/AIDS ,where one could find healthy family members at night, taking care of their relatives dying from possible communicable diseases, without any protection or security. Obviously with vicious malaria carrying mosquitos biting and transfusing blood from both parties at will.

One could tell from the voices of the mental health practitioners present, that the state of mental healthcare in the country is pathetic and less recognized as vital to the total healthcare system.

Despite of medics trained in psychiatry, heading the national health system as Medical Directors, the situation was not improving, furthermore psychiatry nurses were being utilized in other more' prioritized' areas rather than in mental health care.

In this Act ,the rights of the mentally ill person s are recognized, especially the right for representation in legal decision making by their next of kin, partner, parent, guardian ,when they are not able to do so.

The objects and purposes of this Act are stated as –

-Promoting the mental health and well-being of all, including the incidences of mental illness;

Co-ordinating the prevention of mental illness, access to mental health care. treatment and rehabilitation services to persons with mental illness;

-Reducing the impact of mental illness, including the effects of stigma on individuals, family and the community;

-Promoting recovery from mental illnesses.

-Enhancing rehabilitation and integration of person with mental illness into the community;

-Ensuring that the rights of a person with mental illness are protected and safeguarded.

9 CONCLUSIONS

The Kenyan political devolution, gives a better context, in which a sustainable Mental Health System and Policy can be build. The Central Government can establish better information sharing systems, adequate financing, provision of psychotropic drugs, skilled workforce development, system.

While the county governments can concentrate on supervision and service delivery ,maintenance and basic hygiene items financing.

Local community volunteer health workers need to be identified and trained in simple counselling, diagnosis and identification of people suffering from mental disorders.

This can be done in cooperation with user/consumer, and family associations ,schools and such religious organizations, like churches, who are already involved in healthcare provision.

On the availability of mental health personnel, Kenya's Mental Health Personnel is reported to be about 77 consultant psychiatrists, 418 psychiatric nurses and 30 clinical psychologists to serve the entire over 40 million population (KNHCR: 2011p xiii).

WHO;2008:p31, identifies mental and behavioral disorders among global conditions that affect the largest number of persons. at any moment globally.

It also observes that more than a half of people attending primary care clinics have diagnosable mental disorder.

It was estimated by Kenya National Health C.R (2011;3) that up to a quarter of outpatients and almost half of patients in healthcare facilities suffer from some mental and behavioral conditions.

However, up to date information and data on the burden and prevalence of mental and behavioral disorders in Kenyan is inadequate

.

Kiima and Jenkins,(2010) estimates that the probable prevalence of psychosis in the country at 1% of the national population. estimated to be about 48 million in 2017. In general hospital settings, the most frequent diagnosis are depression ,substance abuse, neurotic stress related and anxiety

The prevalence of mental disorders may also be attributed to the noted cases of suicide, homicides and domestic and political /ideological violence.

The traumatic events such as Mau Mau guerilla activities of 1950s; and the brutal colonial villagization and detentions of the communities surrounding Mount Kenya

The Agikuyu, are now the most populous community in Kenya; when one adds the related Ameeru and Aembu, there are more than a quarter of all Kenyans. If one add to their population their linguistic relatives the Akamba, their numerical figure exceeds 40%.

However during the colonial period they were the most traumatized peoples, not only was their land forcefully stolen by the colonialists, but they were to suffer massive dislocations, detentions and villagization and militarized reserves.

They underwent racially color-coded classifications:

Whitish-the colonial loyalists' such as Missionary converts

Blackish- irreconcilable nationalist rebels (Mau-Mau) and the Greyish- in-betweens, who were majority of the population

The colonialists saw everything in terms of black and white and the possible in between., grey.

In 1954, there were over 40 'Agikuyu' concentration and detention camps, following the declaration of emergency, and restrictions of the Agikuyu, and their repatriation to Central Kenya, regardless of their place of birth.

At least, I remember as a young boy running around a barbed wired screening camp, full of naked men and women, including my parents, who had to undergo through the pipeline of classification; fortunate for them they were classified greyish material, that could persuaded through their strong Christian convictions.

However, many of those that were released in similar manner, they had to go back into the villages, with mines and sharpened sticks, and surrounded by lots of barbed wires.

These trenches were dug through slave labor and daily hard working routine ,with lots of spying and security surveillance and by the colonial home guards and their racist commanders.

The British atrocities in Kenya are well documented, and the physical and psychological damages they made to these communities. The colonial treatment of Agikuyu was brutal and geared by racism and terrorism. In reverse the Agikuyu through Mau Mau gave back to the British, what they had created in local communities, thuggery, terrorism and contempt.

Moreover, we cannot forget that during the colonial period one of the Psychiatrist /Medical Officer in charge of the Mathare Mental Hospital was Dr. J. C. Carothers, (1954), who authored of Psychology of the Mau Mau, in which his psychoanalytic views of the Africans demonstrate lack of understanding and the colonial ignorance of the time.

This view seemed to be shared even to an extent, by such anthropologists as Dr. L .S. B. Leakey, whom the Agikuyu trusted, taught their language, underwent their circumcision ritual and made an elder. He was also considered an intelligence informer, giving (mis)information on the Mau Mau to the British colonial operatives and administration.

According to him Africans are mentally disintegrated and lack personal synthetization; they are animal like, just like all other pre-literates.

No wonder complaints have been heard from the patients, about treatments and conditions of the hospital , at times being worse than animal cages.

.Many other terrorist disasters as well as violence and conflicts for example the 2007 and previous pre and post elections politically driven violence and similar conflicts have played significantly to development of post-traumatic disorders, anxiety and depression.

HIV/AIDS is a life threatening and disabling disease. A part of individuals with HIV/AIDS suffer psychological consequences as a result of the infection. Stigma and discrimination against people with HIV/AIDS contributes to psychological stress. Some of the resultant common disorders are anxiety or depressive disorders, adjustment disorders and cognitive deficits (WHO: 2003).

Hopelessness and desperation may partly be attributed to such occurrence. In regard provision of mental health services, Mathari district hospital is the main mental health specialized hospital in Kenya and attends to an average of 1500 in and out patients.

Family members of persons infected also suffer psychologically due to stigma and loss of their family members. In addition, healthy behavior which is dependent on a person's mental health is a determinant of spread of AIDS.

Persons with psychiatric disorders such as depression and substance use disorders are more likely to engage in high risk sexual behavior which exposes them to sexually transmitted diseases such as HIV/AIDS.

10 REFERENCES

Benedict, Ruth, 1934. Patterns of culture.

New York Columbia University Press.

Bernard, C. 1957. An Introduction to the Study of Experimental

Medicine. New York: Dover .

Cannon, W.B. 1939. Wisdom of the Body: New York: Norton.

Darwin, C. 1859. Origin of Species by Means of Natural Selection.

New York: Modern Library.

Elkins, Caroline (2005)Imperial Reckoning; The Untold Story of Britain's Gulag in Kenya. , US ,Henry Holton and Co.

Freud, Anne 1936. The Ego-Id mechanism and Reference. London: Mozart.

Freud, S. 1954. The Origins of Psycho-Analysis: Letters, Drafts and Notes: 1887-1902.

Freud, S. and J. Breuer 1892. On the Theory of Hysterical Attacks Collected Papers 5: 27-30.

Hartmann, H. 1939. Ego psychology and the Problem of Adaption. New York: International University Press

Jenkins, R.; Kima,D.,Njenga,F.,Okonji ,M. Kiogora,J. et al (2010) Integration of Mental Health into Primary Care in Kenya; World Psychiatry 9:118-120)

Leakey, L.S.B. (1937),White African

London: Hodder and Stoughton Ltd.

Leakey, L.S.B. (1952),Mau Mau and the Kikuyu.

London: Methuen &Co. Ltd.

Leakey, L.S.B. (1954), Defeating Mau Mau;

London: Methuen &Co. Ltd.

Pollock, George, H. 1961. "Mourning and Adaptation"

International Journal of Psycho-Analysis 42:341-363.

World Health Organization,(2008) Integrating Mental Health into
Primary Care: A Global Perspective.

World Health Organization,(2009) Mental Health, resilience and inequalities.

World Health Organization(2010), Equity, social determinants and public health programs. .

.

ABOUT THE AUTHOR

The Revd. Prof. Dr. Nehemy Ndirangu Kihara was born in Nanyuki in Laikipia County of Kenya, East Africa.

He was educated at Timau in Meru County and Nairobi before graduating with a Licentiate of Theological Education from St. Paul's University   (United Theological College), Limuru in Kiambu County.

He holds a Bachelor of Theology (B.Th.) in Biblical Literature and Geographic History from Christian International College.

He graduated and attained with honors a Master of Divinity (M.Div.) in Social Ethics, Psychology of Religion and Counseling, from the Interdenominational Theological Center at the Clark Atlanta University Complex.

He also attained a Doctor of Philosophy (Ph.D.) in Anthropology, Sociology of Religion and Political Science from Emory University.

As an Investigative Journalist and Radio Broadcaster this Independent Publisher hosted a weekend English and still hosts a weekly Swahili Community Show for Sagal Radio Services at WATB 1420 AM Station in Decatur, GA.

As an Interdisplinary Educator he taught Security Management and Police Studies for the Institute of Peace and Security Studies, (now known as the Department of Security and Correctional Science) of Kenyatta University in Nanyuki Campus, where he was the Coordinator of Humanities and Examinations Officer.

The Author also taught Introductory Psychology, Sociology, Criminal Procedure and Law of Evidence, Intelligence-Led Policing, Public Administration and General Management Principles among other units at the Nyeri and Embu Campuses.

He was an Adjunct Professor of Sociology/ Social Sciences at the Atlanta Campus of Saint Leo University, Tampa, Fl. Taught such courses as Anthropology, Sociology, and Criminal Justice units as Social Theory, Drugs and Society, Marriage and Family, Research Methods, Human Behavior, among others He was an Adjunct Professor of Ethics at the Georgia Campus (Henry Medical Center) of the College of Health, University of St. Francis, Joliet, Ill.,

The Author was also the founding Moderating Bishop of the Ujamaa Nomadic Church -Without Borders, as a new church- mission initiative in US. He had also been an Urban Renewal/ Organizing Pastor of Beth Salem United Presbyterian Church, Columbus, Georgia. He served as an International Missionary in California, Iowa and New York, under the Mission to US program of the Presbyterian Church, USA.

As a Senior Lecturer at Kenyatta University, the Author taught African Culture, Belief Systems, Social Theory and Research Methods units in the Department of Philosophy and Religious Studies and also in the Department of Sociology.

He is an Activist Scholar, who fought for academic freedom and excellence in Kenya, which led to his unfair dismissal from university teaching ,by the dictatorial Moi government which controlled all public universities and educational institutions.

Reverend Professor Ndirangu Kihara started his career a high school teacher and principal at Muthithi Secondary School, and then an ordained Church Minister of Muthithi Parish and the Stated Clerk of the wider Murang'a Presbytery of the Presbyterian Church of East Africa.

BLUERGREEN PUBLISHING